BUDGET
TRACKER

This Tracker Belongs To:

_____

Tracker Timeline:

_____

REVIVE *stationery*

Budget Tracker

Text edits © 2025 Revive
Design © 2025 Revive

Every reasonable effort has been made to contact the copyright holders of all material reproduced in this book.

ISBN: 978-1-83412-031-7

INDEX

ANNUAL SAVINGS GOAL

COLOR IN YOUR SAVINGS FROM EACH MONTH AND TOTAL IT UP AT THE BOTTOM!

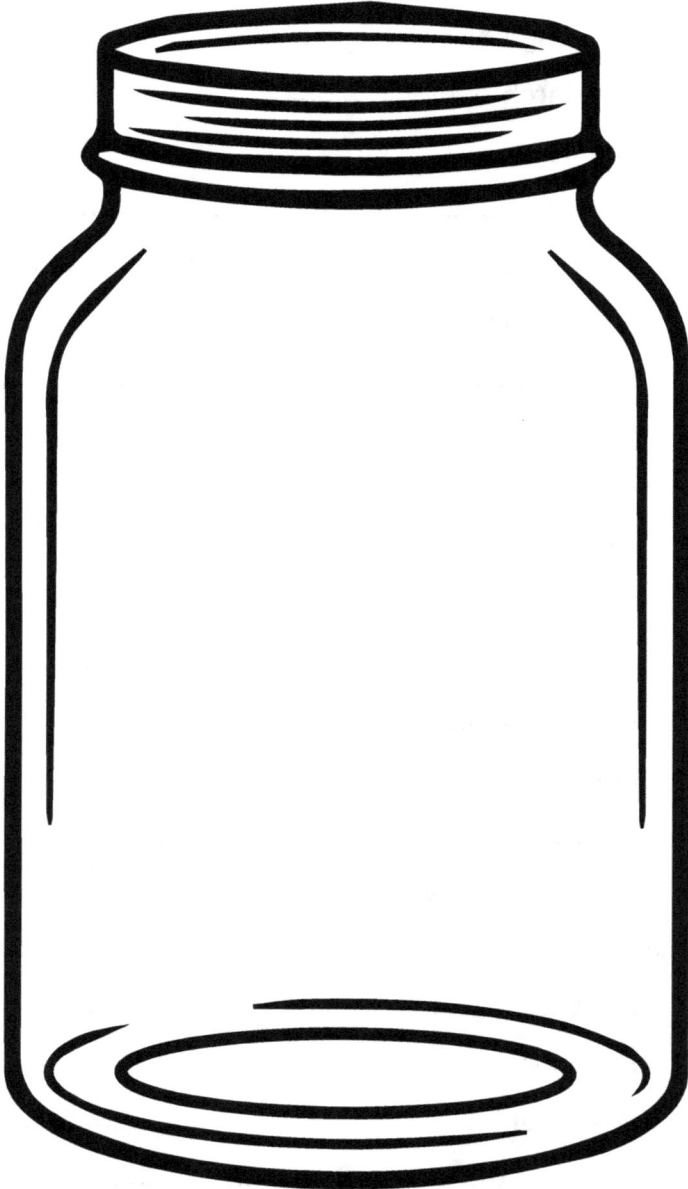

SAVINGS TRACKER

KEEP TRACK OF HOW MUCH
YOU SAVE EACH MONTH

JAN

FEB

MAR

APR

MAY

JUN

JUL

AUG

SEPT

OCT

NOV

DEC

YEARLY SPENDING OVERVIEW

KEEP TRACK OF YOUR OVERALL MONTHLY TRENDS

MONTHLY INCOME	JAN	FEB	MAR	APR	MAY	JUN

EXPENSES	JAN	FEB	MAR	APR	MAY	JUN

YEARLY SPENDING OVERVIEW
KEEP TRACK OF YOUR OVERALL MONTHLY TRENDS

MONTHLY INCOME	JUL	AUG	SEPT	OCT	NOV	DEC

EXPENSES	JUL	AUG	SEPT	OCT	NOV	DEC

JAN - MAR BINGO

CHALLENGE YOURSELF TO SAVE UP TO $500!
COLOR IN ALL SQUARES TO WIN

$15	$2	$75	$20	$15
$1	$3	$4	$20	$3
$5	$50	$2	$10	$5
$2	$8	$50	$5	$25
$50	$25	$75	$25	$5

SAVINGS EARNED:

TIPS, TRICKS, & WAYS TO IMPROVE:

JAN – MAR GOALS

TAKE A MOMENT TO ESTABLISH
YOUR GOALS FOR EACH QUARTER

DESCRIPTION	HABIT	SHORT TERM	MEDIUM TERM	LONG TERM
	☐	☐	☐	☐
	☐	☐	☐	☐
	☐	☐	☐	☐
	☐	☐	☐	☐
	☐	☐	☐	☐
	☐	☐	☐	☐
	☐	☐	☐	☐
	☐	☐	☐	☐
	☐	☐	☐	☐
	☐	☐	☐	☐
	☐	☐	☐	☐
	☐	☐	☐	☐
	☐	☐	☐	☐
	☐	☐	☐	☐
	☐	☐	☐	☐
	☐	☐	☐	☐
	☐	☐	☐	☐

JANUARY

NEW YEAR, NEW BUDGET—START FRESH AND MAKE YOUR MONEY WORK FOR YOU!

MONTHLY CHECKLIST		
DATE	☑	DESCRIPTION
	☐	
	☐	
	☐	
	☐	
	☐	

MONTHLY INCOME		
DATE	DESCRIPTION	AMOUNT
TOTAL INCOME		

MONTHLY SAVINGS		
DATE	DESCRIPTION	AMOUNT
TOTAL SAVINGS		

IMPORTANT DATES						
SUNDAY	MONDAY	TUESDAY	WEDNESDAY	THURSDAY	FRIDAY	SATURDAY

JANUARY

HOUSING/UTILITIES		
DESCRIPTION	BUDGETED	ACTUAL
SUBTOTAL		

TRANSPORTATION		
DESCRIPTION	BUDGETED	ACTUAL
SUBTOTAL		

PERSONAL		
DESCRIPTION	BUDGETED	ACTUAL
SUBTOTAL		

MISCELLANEOUS		
DESCRIPTION	BUDGETED	ACTUAL
SUBTOTAL		

FOOD		
DESCRIPTION	BUDGETED	ACTUAL
SUBTOTAL		

HEALTH		
DESCRIPTION	BUDGETED	ACTUAL
SUBTOTAL		

LIFESTYLE		
DESCRIPTION	BUDGETED	ACTUAL
SUBTOTAL		

DEBTS/LOANS		
DESCRIPTION	BUDGETED	ACTUAL
SUBTOTAL		

BUDGETED	ACTUAL	OVER/UNDER BY

JANUARY RECAP
REFLECT ON YOUR MONTH

OVERVIEW

INCOMING BALANCE	TOTAL INCOME	TOTAL EXPENSES	DEBT PAID	TOTAL SAVINGS	REMAINING BALANCE

DEBT TRACKER

DESCRIPTION	OWED	INTEREST RATE	PAID	OWING

BUDGET BREAKDOWN

CATEGORY	AMOUNT	PERCENTAGE	PORTION OF BUDGET
HOUSING/UTILITIES	$	%	10% 20% 30% 40% 50% 60% 70% 80% 90%
TRANSPORTATION	$	%	10% 20% 30% 40% 50% 60% 70% 80% 90%
PERSONAL	$	%	10% 20% 30% 40% 50% 60% 70% 80% 90%
MISCELLANEOUS	$	%	10% 20% 30% 40% 50% 60% 70% 80% 90%
FOOD	$	%	10% 20% 30% 40% 50% 60% 70% 80% 90%
HEALTH	$	%	10% 20% 30% 40% 50% 60% 70% 80% 90%
DEBT	$	%	10% 20% 30% 40% 50% 60% 70% 80% 90%
LIFESTYLE	$	%	10% 20% 30% 40% 50% 60% 70% 80% 90%

MONTHLY BUDGET SCORE

1	2	3	4	5	6	7	8	9	10

BUDGET LEARNINGS

DO'S	DON'TS

JANUARY NOTES

FEBRUARY

LOVE YOUR FUTURE SELF—SPEND WISELY AND SAVE INTENTIONALLY.

MONTHLY CHECKLIST		
DATE	☑	DESCRIPTION
	☐	
	☐	
	☐	
	☐	
	☐	

MONTHLY INCOME		
DATE	DESCRIPTION	AMOUNT
TOTAL INCOME		

MONTHLY SAVINGS		
DATE	DESCRIPTION	AMOUNT
TOTAL SAVINGS		

IMPORTANT DATES						
SUNDAY	MONDAY	TUESDAY	WEDNESDAY	THURSDAY	FRIDAY	SATURDAY

FEBRUARY

HOUSING/UTILITIES		
DESCRIPTION	BUDGETED	ACTUAL
SUBTOTAL		

TRANSPORTATION		
DESCRIPTION	BUDGETED	ACTUAL
SUBTOTAL		

PERSONAL		
DESCRIPTION	BUDGETED	ACTUAL
SUBTOTAL		

MISCELLANEOUS		
DESCRIPTION	BUDGETED	ACTUAL
SUBTOTAL		

FOOD		
DESCRIPTION	BUDGETED	ACTUAL
SUBTOTAL		

HEALTH		
DESCRIPTION	BUDGETED	ACTUAL
SUBTOTAL		

LIFESTYLE		
DESCRIPTION	BUDGETED	ACTUAL
SUBTOTAL		

DEBTS/LOANS		
DESCRIPTION	BUDGETED	ACTUAL
SUBTOTAL		

BUDGETED	ACTUAL	OVER/UNDER BY

FEBRUARY RECAP
REFLECT ON YOUR MONTH

OVERVIEW					
INCOMING BALANCE	TOTAL INCOME	TOTAL EXPENSES	DEBT PAID	TOTAL SAVINGS	REMAINING BALANCE

DEBT TRACKER				
DESCRIPTION	OWED	INTEREST RATE	PAID	OWING

BUDGET BREAKDOWN			
CATEGORY	AMOUNT	PERCENTAGE	PORTION OF BUDGET
HOUSING/UTILITIES	$	%	10% 20% 30% 40% 50% 60% 70% 80% 90%
TRANSPORTATION	$	%	10% 20% 30% 40% 50% 60% 70% 80% 90%
PERSONAL	$	%	10% 20% 30% 40% 50% 60% 70% 80% 90%
MISCELLANEOUS	$	%	10% 20% 30% 40% 50% 60% 70% 80% 90%
FOOD	$	%	10% 20% 30% 40% 50% 60% 70% 80% 90%
HEALTH	$	%	10% 20% 30% 40% 50% 60% 70% 80% 90%
DEBT	$	%	10% 20% 30% 40% 50% 60% 70% 80% 90%
LIFESTYLE	$	%	10% 20% 30% 40% 50% 60% 70% 80% 90%

MONTHLY BUDGET SCORE									
1	2	3	4	5	6	7	8	9	10

BUDGET LEARNINGS	
DO'S	DON'TS

FEBRUARY NOTES

MARCH

SPRING INTO SMART SPENDING—PRUNE WASTEFUL HABITS AND WATCH YOUR SAVINGS GROW!

MONTHLY CHECKLIST		
DATE	☑	DESCRIPTION
	☐	
	☐	
	☐	
	☐	
	☐	

MONTHLY INCOME		
DATE	DESCRIPTION	AMOUNT
TOTAL INCOME		

MONTHLY SAVINGS		
DATE	DESCRIPTION	AMOUNT
TOTAL SAVINGS		

IMPORTANT DATES						
SUNDAY	MONDAY	TUESDAY	WEDNESDAY	THURSDAY	FRIDAY	SATURDAY

MARCH

HOUSING/UTILITIES		
DESCRIPTION	BUDGETED	ACTUAL
SUBTOTAL		

TRANSPORTATION		
DESCRIPTION	BUDGETED	ACTUAL
SUBTOTAL		

PERSONAL		
DESCRIPTION	BUDGETED	ACTUAL
SUBTOTAL		

MISCELLANEOUS		
DESCRIPTION	BUDGETED	ACTUAL
SUBTOTAL		

FOOD		
DESCRIPTION	BUDGETED	ACTUAL
SUBTOTAL		

HEALTH		
DESCRIPTION	BUDGETED	ACTUAL
SUBTOTAL		

LIFESTYLE		
DESCRIPTION	BUDGETED	ACTUAL
SUBTOTAL		

DEBTS/LOANS		
DESCRIPTION	BUDGETED	ACTUAL
SUBTOTAL		

BUDGETED	ACTUAL	OVER/UNDER BY

MARCH RECAP
REFLECT ON YOUR MONTH

OVERVIEW

INCOMING BALANCE	TOTAL INCOME	TOTAL EXPENSES	DEBT PAID	TOTAL SAVINGS	REMAINING BALANCE

DEBT TRACKER

DESCRIPTION	OWED	INTEREST RATE	PAID	OWING

BUDGET BREAKDOWN

CATEGORY	AMOUNT	PERCENTAGE	PORTION OF BUDGET
HOUSING/UTILITIES	$	%	10% 20% 30% 40% 50% 60% 70% 80% 90%
TRANSPORTATION	$	%	10% 20% 30% 40% 50% 60% 70% 80% 90%
PERSONAL	$	%	10% 20% 30% 40% 50% 60% 70% 80% 90%
MISCELLANEOUS	$	%	10% 20% 30% 40% 50% 60% 70% 80% 90%
FOOD	$	%	10% 20% 30% 40% 50% 60% 70% 80% 90%
HEALTH	$	%	10% 20% 30% 40% 50% 60% 70% 80% 90%
DEBT	$	%	10% 20% 30% 40% 50% 60% 70% 80% 90%
LIFESTYLE	$	%	10% 20% 30% 40% 50% 60% 70% 80% 90%

MONTHLY BUDGET SCORE

1	2	3	4	5	6	7	8	9	10

BUDGET LEARNINGS

DO'S	DON'TS

MARCH NOTES

JAN - MAR RECAP
REFLECT ON YOUR QUARTER

OVERVIEW

MONTH	INCOMING BALANCE	TOTAL INCOME	TOTAL EXPENSES	DEBT PAID	TOTAL SAVINGS	REMAINING BALANCE
JANUARY						
FEBRUARY						
MARCH						

DEBT TRACKER

DESCRIPTION	ON TRACK?	ANY CHANGES?

BUDGET BREAKDOWN

CATEGORY	✓	AMOUNT	PERCENTAGE
HOUSING/UTILITIES	☐	$	%
TRANSPORTATION	☐	$	%
PERSONAL	☐	$	%
MISCELLANEOUS	☐	$	%
FOOD	☐	$	%
HEALTH	☐	$	%
DEBT	☐	$	%
LIFESTYLE	☐	$	%

BUDGET DISTRIBUTION

MONTH-TO-MONTH BUDGET SCORES

MONTHLY BUDGET SCORES

JANUARY   FEBRUARY   MARCH

JAN - MAR NOTES

APR – JUN BINGO

CHALLENGE YOURSELF TO SAVE UP TO $500!
COLOR IN ALL SQUARES TO WIN

$15	$2	$75	$20	$15
$1	$3	$4	$20	$3
$5	$50	$2	$10	$5
$2	$8	$50	$5	$25
$50	$25	$75	$25	$5

SAVINGS EARNED:

TIPS, TRICKS, & WAYS TO IMPROVE:

APR – JUN GOALS
TAKE A MOMENT TO ESTABLISH
YOUR GOALS FOR EACH QUARTER

DESCRIPTION	HABIT	SHORT TERM	MEDIUM TERM	LONG TERM
	☐	☐	☐	☐
	☐	☐	☐	☐
	☐	☐	☐	☐
	☐	☐	☐	☐
	☐	☐	☐	☐
	☐	☐	☐	☐
	☐	☐	☐	☐
	☐	☐	☐	☐
	☐	☐	☐	☐
	☐	☐	☐	☐
	☐	☐	☐	☐
	☐	☐	☐	☐
	☐	☐	☐	☐
	☐	☐	☐	☐
	☐	☐	☐	☐
	☐	☐	☐	☐
	☐	☐	☐	☐

APRIL

TAX SEASON REMINDER: EVERY DOLLAR HAS A JOB—
MAKE SURE YOURS ARE WORKING FOR YOU!

MONTHLY CHECKLIST

DATE	☑	DESCRIPTION
	☐	
	☐	
	☐	
	☐	
	☐	

MONTHLY INCOME

DATE	DESCRIPTION	AMOUNT
TOTAL INCOME		

MONTHLY SAVINGS

DATE	DESCRIPTION	AMOUNT
TOTAL SAVINGS		

IMPORTANT DATES

SUNDAY	MONDAY	TUESDAY	WEDNESDAY	THURSDAY	FRIDAY	SATURDAY

APRIL

HOUSING/UTILITIES

DESCRIPTION	BUDGETED	ACTUAL
SUBTOTAL		

TRANSPORTATION

DESCRIPTION	BUDGETED	ACTUAL
SUBTOTAL		

PERSONAL

DESCRIPTION	BUDGETED	ACTUAL
SUBTOTAL		

MISCELLANEOUS

DESCRIPTION	BUDGETED	ACTUAL
SUBTOTAL		

FOOD

DESCRIPTION	BUDGETED	ACTUAL
SUBTOTAL		

HEALTH

DESCRIPTION	BUDGETED	ACTUAL
SUBTOTAL		

LIFESTYLE

DESCRIPTION	BUDGETED	ACTUAL
SUBTOTAL		

DEBTS/LOANS

DESCRIPTION	BUDGETED	ACTUAL
SUBTOTAL		

BUDGETED	ACTUAL	OVER/UNDER BY

APRIL RECAP
REFLECT ON YOUR MONTH

OVERVIEW					
INCOMING BALANCE	TOTAL INCOME	TOTAL EXPENSES	DEBT PAID	TOTAL SAVINGS	REMAINING BALANCE

DEBT TRACKER				
DESCRIPTION	OWED	INTEREST RATE	PAID	OWING

BUDGET BREAKDOWN			
CATEGORY	AMOUNT	PERCENTAGE	PORTION OF BUDGET
HOUSING/UTILITIES	$	%	10% 20% 30% 40% 50% 60% 70% 80% 90%
TRANSPORTATION	$	%	10% 20% 30% 40% 50% 60% 70% 80% 90%
PERSONAL	$	%	10% 20% 30% 40% 50% 60% 70% 80% 90%
MISCELLANEOUS	$	%	10% 20% 30% 40% 50% 60% 70% 80% 90%
FOOD	$	%	10% 20% 30% 40% 50% 60% 70% 80% 90%
HEALTH	$	%	10% 20% 30% 40% 50% 60% 70% 80% 90%
DEBT	$	%	10% 20% 30% 40% 50% 60% 70% 80% 90%
LIFESTYLE	$	%	10% 20% 30% 40% 50% 60% 70% 80% 90%

MONTHLY BUDGET SCORE									
1	2	3	4	5	6	7	8	9	10

BUDGET LEARNINGS	
DO'S	DON'TS

APRIL NOTES

MAY

MAKE YOUR MONEY BLOOM—
BUDGET TODAY, FLOURISH TOMORROW!

MONTHLY CHECKLIST

DATE	☑	DESCRIPTION
	☐	
	☐	
	☐	
	☐	
	☐	

MONTHLY INCOME

DATE	DESCRIPTION	AMOUNT
TOTAL INCOME		

MONTHLY SAVINGS

DATE	DESCRIPTION	AMOUNT
TOTAL SAVINGS		

IMPORTANT DATES

SUNDAY	MONDAY	TUESDAY	WEDNESDAY	THURSDAY	FRIDAY	SATURDAY

MAY

HOUSING/UTILITIES		
DESCRIPTION	BUDGETED	ACTUAL
SUBTOTAL		

TRANSPORTATION		
DESCRIPTION	BUDGETED	ACTUAL
SUBTOTAL		

PERSONAL		
DESCRIPTION	BUDGETED	ACTUAL
SUBTOTAL		

MISCELLANEOUS		
DESCRIPTION	BUDGETED	ACTUAL
SUBTOTAL		

FOOD		
DESCRIPTION	BUDGETED	ACTUAL
SUBTOTAL		

HEALTH		
DESCRIPTION	BUDGETED	ACTUAL
SUBTOTAL		

LIFESTYLE		
DESCRIPTION	BUDGETED	ACTUAL
SUBTOTAL		

DEBTS/LOANS		
DESCRIPTION	BUDGETED	ACTUAL
SUBTOTAL		

BUDGETED	ACTUAL	OVER/UNDER BY

MAY RECAP

REFLECT ON YOUR MONTH

OVERVIEW

INCOMING BALANCE	TOTAL INCOME	TOTAL EXPENSES	DEBT PAID	TOTAL SAVINGS	REMAINING BALANCE

DEBT TRACKER

DESCRIPTION	OWED	INTEREST RATE	PAID	OWING

BUDGET BREAKDOWN

CATEGORY	AMOUNT	PERCENTAGE	PORTION OF BUDGET
HOUSING/UTILITIES	$	%	10% 20% 30% 40% 50% 60% 70% 80% 90%
TRANSPORTATION	$	%	10% 20% 30% 40% 50% 60% 70% 80% 90%
PERSONAL	$	%	10% 20% 30% 40% 50% 60% 70% 80% 90%
MISCELLANEOUS	$	%	10% 20% 30% 40% 50% 60% 70% 80% 90%
FOOD	$	%	10% 20% 30% 40% 50% 60% 70% 80% 90%
HEALTH	$	%	10% 20% 30% 40% 50% 60% 70% 80% 90%
DEBT	$	%	10% 20% 30% 40% 50% 60% 70% 80% 90%
LIFESTYLE	$	%	10% 20% 30% 40% 50% 60% 70% 80% 90%

MONTHLY BUDGET SCORE

1	2	3	4	5	6	7	8	9	10

BUDGET LEARNINGS

DO'S	DON'TS

MAY NOTES

JUNE

SUMMER FUN DOESN'T HAVE TO BREAK THE BANK— PLAN, SAVE, AND ENJOY!

MONTHLY CHECKLIST

DATE	☑	DESCRIPTION
	☐	
	☐	
	☐	
	☐	
	☐	

MONTHLY INCOME

DATE	DESCRIPTION	AMOUNT
TOTAL INCOME		

MONTHLY SAVINGS

DATE	DESCRIPTION	AMOUNT
TOTAL SAVINGS		

IMPORTANT DATES

SUNDAY	MONDAY	TUESDAY	WEDNESDAY	THURSDAY	FRIDAY	SATURDAY

JUNE

HOUSING/UTILITIES		
DESCRIPTION	BUDGETED	ACTUAL
SUBTOTAL		

TRANSPORTATION		
DESCRIPTION	BUDGETED	ACTUAL
SUBTOTAL		

PERSONAL		
DESCRIPTION	BUDGETED	ACTUAL
SUBTOTAL		

MISCELLANEOUS		
DESCRIPTION	BUDGETED	ACTUAL
SUBTOTAL		

FOOD		
DESCRIPTION	BUDGETED	ACTUAL
SUBTOTAL		

HEALTH		
DESCRIPTION	BUDGETED	ACTUAL
SUBTOTAL		

LIFESTYLE		
DESCRIPTION	BUDGETED	ACTUAL
SUBTOTAL		

DEBTS/LOANS		
DESCRIPTION	BUDGETED	ACTUAL
SUBTOTAL		

BUDGETED	ACTUAL	OVER/UNDER BY

JUNE RECAP
REFLECT ON YOUR MONTH

OVERVIEW

INCOMING BALANCE	TOTAL INCOME	TOTAL EXPENSES	DEBT PAID	TOTAL SAVINGS	REMAINING BALANCE

DEBT TRACKER

DESCRIPTION	OWED	INTEREST RATE	PAID	OWING

BUDGET BREAKDOWN

CATEGORY	AMOUNT	PERCENTAGE	PORTION OF BUDGET
HOUSING/UTILITIES	$	%	10% 20% 30% 40% 50% 60% 70% 80% 90%
TRANSPORTATION	$	%	10% 20% 30% 40% 50% 60% 70% 80% 90%
PERSONAL	$	%	10% 20% 30% 40% 50% 60% 70% 80% 90%
MISCELLANEOUS	$	%	10% 20% 30% 40% 50% 60% 70% 80% 90%
FOOD	$	%	10% 20% 30% 40% 50% 60% 70% 80% 90%
HEALTH	$	%	10% 20% 30% 40% 50% 60% 70% 80% 90%
DEBT	$	%	10% 20% 30% 40% 50% 60% 70% 80% 90%
LIFESTYLE	$	%	10% 20% 30% 40% 50% 60% 70% 80% 90%

MONTHLY BUDGET SCORE

1	2	3	4	5	6	7	8	9	10

BUDGET LEARNINGS

DO'S	DON'TS

JUNE NOTES

APR - JUN RECAP
REFLECT ON YOUR QUARTER

OVERVIEW

MONTH	INCOMING BALANCE	TOTAL INCOME	TOTAL EXPENSES	DEBT PAID	TOTAL SAVINGS	REMAINING BALANCE
APRIL						
MAY						
JUNE						

DEBT TRACKER

DESCRIPTION	ON TRACK?	ANY CHANGES?

BUDGET BREAKDOWN

CATEGORY	✓	AMOUNT	PERCENTAGE
HOUSING/UTILITIES	☐	$	%
TRANSPORTATION	☐	$	%
PERSONAL	☐	$	%
MISCELLANEOUS	☐	$	%
FOOD	☐	$	%
HEALTH	☐	$	%
DEBT	☐	$	%
LIFESTYLE	☐	$	%

BUDGET DISTRIBUTION

MONTH-TO-MONTH BUDGET SCORES

MONTHLY BUDGET SCORES

APRIL   MAY   JUNE

APR - JUN NOTES

JUL – SEPT BINGO

CHALLENGE YOURSELF TO SAVE UP TO $500!
COLOR IN ALL SQUARES TO WIN

$15	$2	$75	$20	$15
$1	$3	$4	$20	$3
$5	$50	$2	$10	$5
$2	$8	$50	$5	$25
$50	$25	$75	$25	$5

SAVINGS EARNED:

_____

TIPS, TRICKS, & WAYS TO IMPROVE:

_____

JUL – SEPT GOALS

TAKE A MOMENT TO ESTABLISH
YOUR GOALS FOR EACH QUARTER

DESCRIPTION	HABIT	SHORT TERM	MEDIUM TERM	LONG TERM
	☐	☐	☐	☐
	☐	☐	☐	☐
	☐	☐	☐	☐
	☐	☐	☐	☐
	☐	☐	☐	☐
	☐	☐	☐	☐
	☐	☐	☐	☐
	☐	☐	☐	☐
	☐	☐	☐	☐
	☐	☐	☐	☐
	☐	☐	☐	☐
	☐	☐	☐	☐
	☐	☐	☐	☐
	☐	☐	☐	☐
	☐	☐	☐	☐
	☐	☐	☐	☐
	☐	☐	☐	☐
	☐	☐	☐	☐

JULY

FINANCIAL FREEDOM IS INDEPENDENCE— BUDGET WISELY AND OWN YOUR FUTURE!

MONTHLY CHECKLIST		
DATE	☑	DESCRIPTION
	☐	
	☐	
	☐	
	☐	
	☐	

MONTHLY INCOME		
DATE	DESCRIPTION	AMOUNT
TOTAL INCOME		

MONTHLY SAVINGS		
DATE	DESCRIPTION	AMOUNT
TOTAL SAVINGS		

IMPORTANT DATES						
SUNDAY	MONDAY	TUESDAY	WEDNESDAY	THURSDAY	FRIDAY	SATURDAY

JULY

HOUSING/UTILITIES		
DESCRIPTION	BUDGETED	ACTUAL
SUBTOTAL		

TRANSPORTATION		
DESCRIPTION	BUDGETED	ACTUAL
SUBTOTAL		

PERSONAL		
DESCRIPTION	BUDGETED	ACTUAL
SUBTOTAL		

MISCELLANEOUS		
DESCRIPTION	BUDGETED	ACTUAL
SUBTOTAL		

FOOD		
DESCRIPTION	BUDGETED	ACTUAL
SUBTOTAL		

HEALTH		
DESCRIPTION	BUDGETED	ACTUAL
SUBTOTAL		

LIFESTYLE		
DESCRIPTION	BUDGETED	ACTUAL
SUBTOTAL		

DEBTS/LOANS		
DESCRIPTION	BUDGETED	ACTUAL
SUBTOTAL		

BUDGETED	ACTUAL	OVER/UNDER BY

JULY RECAP
REFLECT ON YOUR MONTH

OVERVIEW

INCOMING BALANCE	TOTAL INCOME	TOTAL EXPENSES	DEBT PAID	TOTAL SAVINGS	REMAINING BALANCE

DEBT TRACKER

DESCRIPTION	OWED	INTEREST RATE	PAID	OWING

BUDGET BREAKDOWN

CATEGORY	AMOUNT	PERCENTAGE	PORTION OF BUDGET
HOUSING/UTILITIES	$	%	10% 20% 30% 40% 50% 60% 70% 80% 90%
TRANSPORTATION	$	%	10% 20% 30% 40% 50% 60% 70% 80% 90%
PERSONAL	$	%	10% 20% 30% 40% 50% 60% 70% 80% 90%
MISCELLANEOUS	$	%	10% 20% 30% 40% 50% 60% 70% 80% 90%
FOOD	$	%	10% 20% 30% 40% 50% 60% 70% 80% 90%
HEALTH	$	%	10% 20% 30% 40% 50% 60% 70% 80% 90%
DEBT	$	%	10% 20% 30% 40% 50% 60% 70% 80% 90%
LIFESTYLE	$	%	10% 20% 30% 40% 50% 60% 70% 80% 90%

MONTHLY BUDGET SCORE

1	2	3	4	5	6	7	8	9	10

BUDGET LEARNINGS

DO'S	DON'TS

JULY NOTES

AUGUST

BACK TO SCHOOL, BACK TO BUDGETING—
INVEST IN KNOWLEDGE AND FINANCIAL STABILITY!

MONTHLY CHECKLIST

DATE	☑	DESCRIPTION
	☐	
	☐	
	☐	
	☐	
	☐	

MONTHLY INCOME

DATE	DESCRIPTION	AMOUNT
TOTAL INCOME		

MONTHLY SAVINGS

DATE	DESCRIPTION	AMOUNT
TOTAL SAVINGS		

IMPORTANT DATES

SUNDAY	MONDAY	TUESDAY	WEDNESDAY	THURSDAY	FRIDAY	SATURDAY

AUGUST

HOUSING/UTILITIES		
DESCRIPTION	BUDGETED	ACTUAL
SUBTOTAL		

TRANSPORTATION		
DESCRIPTION	BUDGETED	ACTUAL
SUBTOTAL		

PERSONAL		
DESCRIPTION	BUDGETED	ACTUAL
SUBTOTAL		

MISCELLANEOUS		
DESCRIPTION	BUDGETED	ACTUAL
SUBTOTAL		

FOOD		
DESCRIPTION	BUDGETED	ACTUAL
SUBTOTAL		

HEALTH		
DESCRIPTION	BUDGETED	ACTUAL
SUBTOTAL		

LIFESTYLE		
DESCRIPTION	BUDGETED	ACTUAL
SUBTOTAL		

DEBTS/LOANS		
DESCRIPTION	BUDGETED	ACTUAL
SUBTOTAL		

BUDGETED	ACTUAL	OVER/UNDER BY

AUGUST RECAP
REFLECT ON YOUR MONTH

OVERVIEW					
INCOMING BALANCE	TOTAL INCOME	TOTAL EXPENSES	DEBT PAID	TOTAL SAVINGS	REMAINING BALANCE

DEBT TRACKER				
DESCRIPTION	OWED	INTEREST RATE	PAID	OWING

BUDGET BREAKDOWN			
CATEGORY	AMOUNT	PERCENTAGE	PORTION OF BUDGET
HOUSING/UTILITIES	$	%	10% 20% 30% 40% 50% 60% 70% 80% 90%
TRANSPORTATION	$	%	10% 20% 30% 40% 50% 60% 70% 80% 90%
PERSONAL	$	%	10% 20% 30% 40% 50% 60% 70% 80% 90%
MISCELLANEOUS	$	%	10% 20% 30% 40% 50% 60% 70% 80% 90%
FOOD	$	%	10% 20% 30% 40% 50% 60% 70% 80% 90%
HEALTH	$	%	10% 20% 30% 40% 50% 60% 70% 80% 90%
DEBT	$	%	10% 20% 30% 40% 50% 60% 70% 80% 90%
LIFESTYLE	$	%	10% 20% 30% 40% 50% 60% 70% 80% 90%

MONTHLY BUDGET SCORE									
1	2	3	4	5	6	7	8	9	10

BUDGET LEARNINGS	
DO'S	DON'TS

AUGUST NOTES

SEPTEMBER

FALL INTO GOOD HABITS—
BUDGETING TODAY MEANS SECURITY TOMORROW.

MONTHLY CHECKLIST		
DATE	☑	DESCRIPTION
	☐	
	☐	
	☐	
	☐	
	☐	

MONTHLY INCOME		
DATE	DESCRIPTION	AMOUNT
TOTAL INCOME		

MONTHLY SAVINGS		
DATE	DESCRIPTION	AMOUNT
TOTAL SAVINGS		

IMPORTANT DATES						
SUNDAY	MONDAY	TUESDAY	WEDNESDAY	THURSDAY	FRIDAY	SATURDAY

SEPTEMBER

HOUSING/UTILITIES

DESCRIPTION	BUDGETED	ACTUAL
SUBTOTAL		

TRANSPORTATION

DESCRIPTION	BUDGETED	ACTUAL
SUBTOTAL		

PERSONAL

DESCRIPTION	BUDGETED	ACTUAL
SUBTOTAL		

MISCELLANEOUS

DESCRIPTION	BUDGETED	ACTUAL
SUBTOTAL		

FOOD

DESCRIPTION	BUDGETED	ACTUAL
SUBTOTAL		

HEALTH

DESCRIPTION	BUDGETED	ACTUAL
SUBTOTAL		

LIFESTYLE

DESCRIPTION	BUDGETED	ACTUAL
SUBTOTAL		

DEBTS/LOANS

DESCRIPTION	BUDGETED	ACTUAL
SUBTOTAL		

BUDGETED	ACTUAL	OVER/UNDER BY

SEPTEMBER RECAP
REFLECT ON YOUR MONTH

OVERVIEW					
INCOMING BALANCE	TOTAL INCOME	TOTAL EXPENSES	DEBT PAID	TOTAL SAVINGS	REMAINING BALANCE

DEBT TRACKER				
DESCRIPTION	OWED	INTEREST RATE	PAID	OWING

BUDGET BREAKDOWN			
CATEGORY	AMOUNT	PERCENTAGE	PORTION OF BUDGET
HOUSING/UTILITIES	$	%	10% 20% 30% 40% 50% 60% 70% 80% 90%
TRANSPORTATION	$	%	10% 20% 30% 40% 50% 60% 70% 80% 90%
PERSONAL	$	%	10% 20% 30% 40% 50% 60% 70% 80% 90%
MISCELLANEOUS	$	%	10% 20% 30% 40% 50% 60% 70% 80% 90%
FOOD	$	%	10% 20% 30% 40% 50% 60% 70% 80% 90%
HEALTH	$	%	10% 20% 30% 40% 50% 60% 70% 80% 90%
DEBT	$	%	10% 20% 30% 40% 50% 60% 70% 80% 90%
LIFESTYLE	$	%	10% 20% 30% 40% 50% 60% 70% 80% 90%

MONTHLY BUDGET SCORE									
1	2	3	4	5	6	7	8	9	10

BUDGET LEARNINGS	
DO'S	DON'TS

SEPTEMBER NOTES

JUL – SEPT RECAP
REFLECT ON YOUR QUARTER

OVERVIEW

MONTH	INCOMING BALANCE	TOTAL INCOME	TOTAL EXPENSES	DEBT PAID	TOTAL SAVINGS	REMAINING BALANCE
JULY						
AUGUST						
SEPTEMBER						

DEBT TRACKER

DESCRIPTION	ON TRACK?	ANY CHANGES?

BUDGET BREAKDOWN

CATEGORY	✓	AMOUNT	PERCENTAGE
HOUSING/UTILITIES	☐	$	%
TRANSPORTATION	☐	$	%
PERSONAL	☐	$	%
MISCELLANEOUS	☐	$	%
FOOD	☐	$	%
HEALTH	☐	$	%
DEBT	☐	$	%
LIFESTYLE	☐	$	%

BUDGET DISTRIBUTION

100%
90%
80%
70%
60%
50%
40%
30%
20%
10%
0%

MONTH-TO-MONTH BUDGET SCORES

MONTHLY BUDGET SCORES

1 2 3 4 5 6 7 8 9 10

JULY   AUGUST   SEPTEMBER

JUL - SEPT NOTES

OCT - DEC BINGO

CHALLENGE YOURSELF TO SAVE UP TO $500!
COLOR IN ALL SQUARES TO WIN

$15	$2	$75	$20	$15
$1	$3	$4	$20	$3
$5	$50	$2	$10	$5
$2	$8	$50	$5	$25
$50	$25	$75	$25	$5

SAVINGS EARNED:

TIPS, TRICKS, & WAYS TO IMPROVE:

OCT - DEC GOALS
TAKE A MOMENT TO ESTABLISH
YOUR GOALS FOR EACH QUARTER

DESCRIPTION	HABIT	SHORT TERM	MEDIUM TERM	LONG TERM
	☐	☐	☐	☐
	☐	☐	☐	☐
	☐	☐	☐	☐
	☐	☐	☐	☐
	☐	☐	☐	☐
	☐	☐	☐	☐
	☐	☐	☐	☐
	☐	☐	☐	☐
	☐	☐	☐	☐
	☐	☐	☐	☐
	☐	☐	☐	☐
	☐	☐	☐	☐
	☐	☐	☐	☐
	☐	☐	☐	☐
	☐	☐	☐	☐
	☐	☐	☐	☐
	☐	☐	☐	☐

OCTOBER

DON'T LET SPOOKY SPENDING HAUNT YOUR FUTURE—
TREAT YOUR SAVINGS, DON'T TRICK YOURSELF!

MONTHLY CHECKLIST

DATE	☑	DESCRIPTION
	☐	
	☐	
	☐	
	☐	
	☐	

MONTHLY INCOME

DATE	DESCRIPTION	AMOUNT
TOTAL INCOME		

MONTHLY SAVINGS

DATE	DESCRIPTION	AMOUNT
TOTAL SAVINGS		

IMPORTANT DATES

SUNDAY	MONDAY	TUESDAY	WEDNESDAY	THURSDAY	FRIDAY	SATURDAY

OCTOBER

HOUSING/UTILITIES		
DESCRIPTION	BUDGETED	ACTUAL
SUBTOTAL		

TRANSPORTATION		
DESCRIPTION	BUDGETED	ACTUAL
SUBTOTAL		

PERSONAL		
DESCRIPTION	BUDGETED	ACTUAL
SUBTOTAL		

MISCELLANEOUS		
DESCRIPTION	BUDGETED	ACTUAL
SUBTOTAL		

FOOD		
DESCRIPTION	BUDGETED	ACTUAL
SUBTOTAL		

HEALTH		
DESCRIPTION	BUDGETED	ACTUAL
SUBTOTAL		

LIFESTYLE		
DESCRIPTION	BUDGETED	ACTUAL
SUBTOTAL		

DEBTS/LOANS		
DESCRIPTION	BUDGETED	ACTUAL
SUBTOTAL		

BUDGETED	ACTUAL	OVER/UNDER BY

OCTOBER RECAP
REFLECT ON YOUR MONTH

OVERVIEW

INCOMING BALANCE	TOTAL INCOME	TOTAL EXPENSES	DEBT PAID	TOTAL SAVINGS	REMAINING BALANCE

DEBT TRACKER

DESCRIPTION	OWED	INTEREST RATE	PAID	OWING

BUDGET BREAKDOWN

CATEGORY	AMOUNT	PERCENTAGE	PORTION OF BUDGET
HOUSING/UTILITIES	$	%	10% 20% 30% 40% 50% 60% 70% 80% 90%
TRANSPORTATION	$	%	10% 20% 30% 40% 50% 60% 70% 80% 90%
PERSONAL	$	%	10% 20% 30% 40% 50% 60% 70% 80% 90%
MISCELLANEOUS	$	%	10% 20% 30% 40% 50% 60% 70% 80% 90%
FOOD	$	%	10% 20% 30% 40% 50% 60% 70% 80% 90%
HEALTH	$	%	10% 20% 30% 40% 50% 60% 70% 80% 90%
DEBT	$	%	10% 20% 30% 40% 50% 60% 70% 80% 90%
LIFESTYLE	$	%	10% 20% 30% 40% 50% 60% 70% 80% 90%

MONTHLY BUDGET SCORE

1	2	3	4	5	6	7	8	9	10

BUDGET LEARNINGS

DO'S	DON'TS

OCTOBER NOTES

NOVEMBER

GRATITUDE AND GOALS—BE THANKFUL FOR WHAT YOU HAVE AND PLAN FOR WHAT YOU WANT.

MONTHLY CHECKLIST

DATE	☑	DESCRIPTION
	☐	
	☐	
	☐	
	☐	
	☐	

MONTHLY INCOME

DATE	DESCRIPTION	AMOUNT
TOTAL INCOME		

MONTHLY SAVINGS

DATE	DESCRIPTION	AMOUNT
TOTAL SAVINGS		

IMPORTANT DATES

SUNDAY	MONDAY	TUESDAY	WEDNESDAY	THURSDAY	FRIDAY	SATURDAY

NOVEMBER

HOUSING/UTILITIES		
DESCRIPTION	BUDGETED	ACTUAL
SUBTOTAL		

TRANSPORTATION		
DESCRIPTION	BUDGETED	ACTUAL
SUBTOTAL		

PERSONAL		
DESCRIPTION	BUDGETED	ACTUAL
SUBTOTAL		

MISCELLANEOUS		
DESCRIPTION	BUDGETED	ACTUAL
SUBTOTAL		

FOOD		
DESCRIPTION	BUDGETED	ACTUAL
SUBTOTAL		

HEALTH		
DESCRIPTION	BUDGETED	ACTUAL
SUBTOTAL		

LIFESTYLE		
DESCRIPTION	BUDGETED	ACTUAL
SUBTOTAL		

DEBTS/LOANS		
DESCRIPTION	BUDGETED	ACTUAL
SUBTOTAL		

BUDGETED	ACTUAL	OVER/UNDER BY

NOVEMBER RECAP

REFLECT ON YOUR MONTH

OVERVIEW					
INCOMING BALANCE	TOTAL INCOME	TOTAL EXPENSES	DEBT PAID	TOTAL SAVINGS	REMAINING BALANCE

DEBT TRACKER				
DESCRIPTION	OWED	INTEREST RATE	PAID	OWING

BUDGET BREAKDOWN			
CATEGORY	AMOUNT	PERCENTAGE	PORTION OF BUDGET
HOUSING/UTILITIES	$	%	10% 20% 30% 40% 50% 60% 70% 80% 90%
TRANSPORTATION	$	%	10% 20% 30% 40% 50% 60% 70% 80% 90%
PERSONAL	$	%	10% 20% 30% 40% 50% 60% 70% 80% 90%
MISCELLANEOUS	$	%	10% 20% 30% 40% 50% 60% 70% 80% 90%
FOOD	$	%	10% 20% 30% 40% 50% 60% 70% 80% 90%
HEALTH	$	%	10% 20% 30% 40% 50% 60% 70% 80% 90%
DEBT	$	%	10% 20% 30% 40% 50% 60% 70% 80% 90%
LIFESTYLE	$	%	10% 20% 30% 40% 50% 60% 70% 80% 90%

MONTHLY BUDGET SCORE									
1	2	3	4	5	6	7	8	9	10

BUDGET LEARNINGS	
DO'S	DON'TS

NOVEMBER NOTES

DECEMBER

GIVE YOURSELF THE GIFT OF FINANCIAL PEACE— BUDGET NOW, STRESS LESS LATER!

MONTHLY CHECKLIST

DATE	☑	DESCRIPTION
	☐	
	☐	
	☐	
	☐	
	☐	

MONTHLY INCOME

DATE	DESCRIPTION	AMOUNT
TOTAL INCOME		

MONTHLY SAVINGS

DATE	DESCRIPTION	AMOUNT
TOTAL SAVINGS		

IMPORTANT DATES

SUNDAY	MONDAY	TUESDAY	WEDNESDAY	THURSDAY	FRIDAY	SATURDAY

DECEMBER

HOUSING/UTILITIES		
DESCRIPTION	BUDGETED	ACTUAL
SUBTOTAL		

TRANSPORTATION		
DESCRIPTION	BUDGETED	ACTUAL
SUBTOTAL		

PERSONAL		
DESCRIPTION	BUDGETED	ACTUAL
SUBTOTAL		

MISCELLANEOUS		
DESCRIPTION	BUDGETED	ACTUAL
SUBTOTAL		

FOOD		
DESCRIPTION	BUDGETED	ACTUAL
SUBTOTAL		

HEALTH		
DESCRIPTION	BUDGETED	ACTUAL
SUBTOTAL		

LIFESTYLE		
DESCRIPTION	BUDGETED	ACTUAL
SUBTOTAL		

DEBTS/LOANS		
DESCRIPTION	BUDGETED	ACTUAL
SUBTOTAL		

BUDGETED	ACTUAL	OVER/UNDER BY

DECEMBER RECAP
REFLECT ON YOUR MONTH

OVERVIEW					
INCOMING BALANCE	TOTAL INCOME	TOTAL EXPENSES	DEBT PAID	TOTAL SAVINGS	REMAINING BALANCE

DEBT TRACKER				
DESCRIPTION	OWED	INTEREST RATE	PAID	OWING

BUDGET BREAKDOWN			
CATEGORY	AMOUNT	PERCENTAGE	PORTION OF BUDGET
HOUSING/UTILITIES	$	%	10% 20% 30% 40% 50% 60% 70% 80% 90%
TRANSPORTATION	$	%	10% 20% 30% 40% 50% 60% 70% 80% 90%
PERSONAL	$	%	10% 20% 30% 40% 50% 60% 70% 80% 90%
MISCELLANEOUS	$	%	10% 20% 30% 40% 50% 60% 70% 80% 90%
FOOD	$	%	10% 20% 30% 40% 50% 60% 70% 80% 90%
HEALTH	$	%	10% 20% 30% 40% 50% 60% 70% 80% 90%
DEBT	$	%	10% 20% 30% 40% 50% 60% 70% 80% 90%
LIFESTYLE	$	%	10% 20% 30% 40% 50% 60% 70% 80% 90%

MONTHLY BUDGET SCORE									
1	2	3	4	5	6	7	8	9	10

BUDGET LEARNINGS	
DO'S	DON'TS

DECEMBER NOTES

OCT - DEC RECAP
REFLECT ON YOUR QUARTER

OVERVIEW

MONTH	INCOMING BALANCE	TOTAL INCOME	TOTAL EXPENSES	DEBT PAID	TOTAL SAVINGS	REMAINING BALANCE
OCTOBER						
NOVEMBER						
DECEMBER						

DEBT TRACKER

DESCRIPTION	ON TRACK?	ANY CHANGES?

BUDGET BREAKDOWN

CATEGORY	✓	AMOUNT	PERCENTAGE
HOUSING/UTILITIES	☐	$	%
TRANSPORTATION	☐	$	%
PERSONAL	☐	$	%
MISCELLANEOUS	☐	$	%
FOOD	☐	$	%
HEALTH	☐	$	%
DEBT	☐	$	%
LIFESTYLE	☐	$	%

BUDGET DISTRIBUTION

100%
90%
80%
70%
60%
50%
40%
30%
20%
10%
0%

MONTH-TO-MONTH BUDGET SCORES

MONTHLY BUDGET SCORES

10
9
8
7
6
5
4
3
2
1

OCTOBER   NOVEMBER   DECEMBER

OCT - DEC NOTES

YEAR IN REVIEW
REFLECT ON YOUR YEAR

BUDGET SCORES

MONTHLY BUDGET SCORES

10
9
8
7
6
5
4
3
2
1

JANUARY   FEBRUARY   MARCH   APRIL   MAY   JUNE

THINGS I DID WELL

_____

_____

_____

_____

_____

_____

_____

_____

_____

_____

_____

_____

_____

_____

_____

YEAR IN REVIEW
REFLECT ON YOUR YEAR

BUDGET SCORES

MONTHLY BUDGET SCORES

10 9 8 7 6 5 4 3 2 1

JULY   AUGUST   SEPTEMBER   OCTOBER   NOVEMBER   DECEMBER

THINGS I SHOULD STOP

_____

_____

_____

_____

_____

_____

_____

_____

_____

_____

_____

_____

_____

YEAR IN REVIEW
REFLECT ON YOUR YEAR

BUDGET SCORES

MONTHLY BUDGET SCORES

10 9 8 7 6 5 4 3 2 1

JANUARY FEBRUARY MARCH APRIL MAY JUNE

THINGS I SHOULD IMPROVE

YEAR IN REVIEW

REFLECT ON YOUR YEAR

BUDGET SCORES

MONTHLY BUDGET SCORES

10 9 8 7 6 5 4 3 2 1

JULY   AUGUST   SEPTEMBER   OCTOBER   NOVEMBER   DECEMBER

THINGS I SHOULD TRY

NOTES

NOTES

NOTES

NOTES

NOTES

NOTES

NOTES

NOTES

NOTES

NOTES

www.ingramcontent.com/pod-product-compliance
Lightning Source LLC
Chambersburg PA
CBHW050557280326
41933CB00011B/1881